SULL
FLUFFYTOES
Finds His Forever Home

Angela Fischels

ANGELA FISCHELS
ILLUSTRATIONS BY NATHAN HAGARTY

Outskirts Press, Inc.
http://www.outskirtspress.com

Paperback ISBN: 978-1-9772-3304-2
Hardback ISBN: 978-1-9772-3180-2

Illustrations by Nathan Hagarty

Outskirts Press and the "OP" logo are trademarks belonging to Outskirts Press, Inc.

PRINTED IN THE UNITED STATES OF AMERICA

This Book Belongs to:

_____

S ullivan P. Fluffytoes wasn't always Sullivan P. Fluffytoes. He was born on a damp spring day on a hobby farm in Minnesota, along with his five brothers. He

couldn't yet open his eyes but he could feel the warmth of his mother's coat and hear the gentle pitter patter of rain on the roof.

In a few days, his eyes opened, and he was delighted to see all his brothers and the new world around him. His brothers of course were equally amused by each new discovery they made. He was a happy kitten and loved to tumble with his siblings. When they grew

tired they would all pile together and sleep in the comfort of their mother's bed. Each day was full of happiness and surprises.

One day, a woman came to their home. She watched the kittens play. She smiled. She seemed very nice, and then she picked up one of his brothers and took him away. All of the others were confused. "Why mother? They asked. "Where are they going?" "You are getting older now, and it is time you are all adopted and start a new life with humans" she gently replied. "Your human will love you and take care of you so don't be sad."

One by one, all the brothers were adopted. "Why doesn't a human want me Mama?" Asked Sullivan P. Fluffytoes (before he was Sullivan P. Fluffytoes). "My darling boy, you are a very special

kitten. When you were born, your heart wasn't strong like your brothers. You may not be able to run as long and far as they can, but your heart is bigger than theirs, and someone will see how wonderful you are. You'll see."

Days passed yet no one came. Sullivan P. Fluffytoes loved his mother very much, but he was sad no human had come to adopt him. One Sunday afternoon, while sleeping in a warm sunbeam, he felt a gentle rub on his belly. And just like that,

he started to purr, deep and loud. He raised his paws to the sky and started to knead them, stretching his toes out wide, before curling them back into his palm. Sullivan P. Fluffytoes (before he was Sullivan P. Fluffytoes) opened his eyes and saw an inviting smile, and kind eyes looking back at him. The woman picked him up and placed him in a carrier. He looked out at his

mother who was rubbing her cheek along the carrier door, carefully placing her scent to comfort his journey. "Good Bye Mother", cried Sullivan P. Fluffytoes (before he was Sullivan P. Fluffytoes). "Be well my sweet boy" she gently replied.

The car ride to his new home was filled with nervous anticipation. An

entire world flew by as he peered through the car window from the safety of his enclosure. He let out a soft meow. After a short while, the car ride ended and he was carried indoors. His travel carrier door opened, and he stepped out. Was this his forever home? There was so much to see and explore, so

he took off running and didn't stop. He ran into the living room. He ran into the kitchen. He ran down the carpeted stairs to the front door. He ran back up the stairs and ran into the bedroom. His new human picked him up, nuzzled his belly and kissed him on his head. "I love you so much Sullivan P. Fluffytoes. An amazing boy like you deserves a grand name!"

Is it really true? wonders Sullivan P. Fluffytoes (who is now Sullivan P. Fluffytoes). Is this my home? Is this my glorious name? Is this my very own human, to keep?

Sullivan P. Fluffytoes and his human played all day. She threw yummy smelling fur mice across

the floor, and he gleefully made chase and brought them back to her. He jumped in the air to catch feathers tethered by string. But, his favorite game was climbing the curtains. Higher and higher he went. He shuttled up and down the cloth pieces like a ninja. His human did not like this game, but she laughed all the same.

Sullivan P. Fluffytoes was tired, and so was his human. She picked him up and placed him next to her on the bed. He was so excited. Too excited to sleep!

"Good night Sullivan P. Fluffytoes. I'll see you in the morning."

"Tomorrow! It was true!" He started to purr, deep and loud. He laid down his heavy head in the warmth of his new bed, in his new forever home.

CPSIA information can be obtained
at www.ICGtesting.com
Printed in the USA
LVHW071625090423
743882LV00016B/191